Bond

English
Assessment Papers

8–9 years

J M Bond
Sarah Lindsay

OXFORD
UNIVERSITY PRESS

OXFORD
UNIVERSITY PRESS

Great Clarendon Street, Oxford, OX2 6DP, United Kingdom

Oxford University Press is a department of the University of Oxford. It furthers the University's objective of excellence in research, scholarship, and education by publishing worldwide. Oxford is a registered trade mark of Oxford University Press in the UK and in certain other countries

© J M Bond and Sarah Lindsay 2002, 2007, 2013

The moral rights of the authors have been asserted

First published in 1973 by Thomas Nelson and Sons Ltd
This edition published in 2014

All rights reserved. No part of this publication may be reproduced, stored in a retrieval system, or transmitted, in any form or by any means, without the prior permission in writing of Oxford University Press, or as expressly permitted by law, by licence or under terms agreed with the appropriate reprographics rights organization. Enquiries concerning reproduction outside the scope of the above should be sent to the Rights Department, Oxford University Press, at the address above.

You must not circulate this work in any other form and you must impose this same condition on any acquirer

British Library Cataloguing in Publication Data
Data available

978-1-4085-2512-8

10 9 8 7 6 5 4 3 2 1

Printed in China

Acknowledgements

Page make-up by OKS Prepress, India
Illustrations by Nigel Kitching, K Kett and Beverly Curl

We are grateful for permission to reprint extracts from the following copyright material:

Pp5-6 extract from *A House Called Awful End* by Philip Ardagh, copyright © 2002, published by Scholastic Ltd. Reprinted with permission by Faber and Faber Ltd and Henry Holt; p18 extract from *The Seven Voyages of Sinbad the Sailor* by John Yeoman, copyright © 2003, Chrysalis Children's Books; pp21-22 extract from *Blitz* © The Estate of Robert Westall 1994 reproduced by permission of Laura Cecil Literary Agency; p25 'Zanzibar' from *Walking on Air* by Berlie Doherty © 1993 Hodder Children's Books, reproduced by permission of David Higham Associates; p30 'Stopping by Woods on a Snowy Evening' from *The Poetry of Robert Frost* edited by Edward Connery Latham, published by Jonathan Cape. Reproduced by permission of the Random House Group Ltd; p36 extract from *Traitor* by Pete Johnson, published by Corgi Yearling. Reprinted by permission of the Random House Group Ltd; p39 extract from *The Copper Treasure* by Melvin Burgess published by A&C Black; pp45-46 extract from *Beaver Towers* by Nigel Hinton © 1995 Nigel Hinton. Reprinted by permission of Penguin Books Ltd; p52 'Billy Doesn't Like School Really' by Paul Cookson. Reproduced with permission of the author; pp55-56 'Ghost soup' from Kingfisher Treasury of Spooky Stories. Copyright © Kingfisher Publications Plc. Reproduced by permission of the publisher, all rights reserved.

Although we have made every effort to trace and contact all copyright holders before publication this has not been possible in all cases. If notified, the publisher will rectify any errors or omissions at the earliest opportunity.

Before you get started

What is Bond?

This book is part of the Bond Assessment Papers series for English, which provides **thorough and continuous practice of key English skills** from ages five to thirteen. Bond's English resources are ideal preparation for many different kinds of test and exam – from SATs to 11+ and other secondary school selection exams.

What does this book cover?

It practises comprehension, spelling, grammar, punctuation and vocabulary work appropriate for children of this age. It is fully in line with the National Curriculum for English and the National Literacy Strategy. One of the key features of Bond Assessment Papers is that each one practises **a wide variety of skills and question types** so that children are always challenged to think – and don't get bored repeating the same question type again and again. We think that variety is the key to effective learning. It helps children 'think on their feet' and cope with the unexpected.

The age given on the cover is for guidance only. As the papers are designed to be reasonably challenging for the age group, any one child may naturally find him or herself working above or below the stated age. The important thing is that children are always encouraged by their performance. Working at the right level is the key to this.

What does the book contain?

- **20 papers** – each one contains 40 questions.
- **Scoring devices** – there are score boxes in the margins and a Progress Chart on page 68. The chart is a visual and motivating way for children to see how they are doing. Encouraging them to colour in the chart as they go along and to try to beat their last score can be highly effective!
- **Next Steps** – advice on what to do after finishing the papers can be found on the inside back cover.
- **Answers** – located in an easily-removed central pull-out section.
- **Key English words** – on page 1 you will find a glossary of special key words that are used in the papers. These are highlighted in bold each time that they appear. These words are now used in the English curriculum and children are expected to know them at this age.

How can you use this book?

One of the great strengths of Bond Assessment Papers is their flexibility. They can be used at home, school and by tutors to:

- provide regular English practice in **bite-sized chunks**
- **highlight strengths and weaknesses** in the core skills
- identify **individual needs**
- set **homework**
- set **timed formal practice** tests – allow about 30 minutes.

It is best to start at the beginning and work though the papers in order.

What does a score mean and how can it be improved?

If children colour in the Progress Chart at the back, this will give an idea of how they are doing. The Next Steps inside the back cover will help you to decide what to do next to help a child progress. We suggest that it is always valuable to go over any wrong answers with children.

Don't forget the website…!

Visit www.bond11plus.co.uk for lots of advice, information and suggestions on everything to do with Bond and helping children to do their best.

Key words

adjectival phrase	a group of words describing a noun
adjective	a word that describes someone or something
adverb	a word that gives extra meaning to a verb
adverbial phrase	a word or phrase that makes the meaning of a verb, adjective or another adverb more specific, for example The Cheshire cat vanished quite slowly beginning with the end of its tail.
alphabetical order	the order found in the alphabet
antonym	a word with a meaning opposite to another word *hot – cold*
collective noun	a word referring to a group *swarm*
compound word	a word made up of two other words *football*
conjunction	a word used to link sentences, phrases and words *and*, *but*
consonant letters	all letters of the alphabet apart from a, e, i, o, u (vowel letters)
contraction	two words shortened into one with an apostrophe placed where the letter/s have been dropped *do not = don't*
definition	the meaning of a word
diminutive	a word implying smallness *booklet*
fronted adverbial	an adverbial that has been moved before the verb, for example The day after tomorrow I'm going on holiday.
homonym	a word that has the same spelling as another word, but a different meaning turn *left*, we *left* the room
homophone	a word that has the same sound as another, but a different meaning or spelling *right / write*
noun	a word for someone or something
past tense	form of a verb showing something that has already happened
personal pronoun	a pronoun used when writing about ourselves or others *I*, *you*, *he*
phrase	a group of words that act as a unit
plural	more than one *cats*
prefix	a group of letters added to the beginning of a word *un*, *dis*
present tense	form of a verb showing something happening now
pronoun	a word often replacing a noun
proper noun	the name of a person, place etc. *Ben*
root word	a word to which prefixes or suffixes can be added to make other words *quickly*
singular	one *cat*
suffix	a group of letters added to the end of a word *ly, ful*
syllables	the beats in a word
synonym	a word with a very similar meaning to another word *quick – fast*
verb	a 'doing' or 'being' word
vowel letters	the letters a, e, i, o, u

Paper 1

Rainforests

Tropical rainforests provide the richest habitat on Earth for living things. They only cover 11 per cent of the planet's land surface but contain over half its plant and animal species. Rainforests are found around the Equator, in regions with a hot temperature all the year round and heavy daily rainfall. The rainforests are found in South America, Central Africa, South Asia and the Pacific islands.

The rainforest grows in a series of layers, reaching up to the light. Trees can grow to heights of 25–45 metres. Their tops form the canopy, which acts as a ceiling for the whole forest. It shields the forest against soil erosion from heavy rain. Some individual trees grow above the canopy to form an emergent layer. The further down the forest you go, the darker it gets. Only 2 per cent of sunlight actually reaches the ground because of the thick vegetation higher up.

Each layer supports its own special range of species. The canopy provides a home for brightly coloured birds, such as toucans and macaws, and a few mammals, such as sloths and monkeys. The layer below is called the understory. Birds, butterflies, snakes and frogs inhabit this layer. Between the understory and the forest floor, lies the shrub layer. This is made up of ferns and small shrubs. The forest floor itself is the place where all the dead plants and leaves rot down to make the soil that keeps the forest alive. The larger animals live here: leopards and gorillas in Africa, tigers and elephants in Asia, tapirs and jaguars in South America.

The rainforest is very fragile. It depends on the thin layer of soil for its food. If the trees are cut down, the soil quickly becomes barren and unable to support plant life again. It reverts to desert. At present the rainforests are being destroyed at an alarming rate for timber. Perhaps 50 rainforest species are becoming extinct every day. The tribal people who live in the forests are being displaced. Forest destruction is one cause of the warming of the whole planet.

Underline the right answers.

1. Which of these continents does not contain rainforests?
   (Asia, Africa, <u>Europe</u>, South America)
2. Which of these species live in the understory?
   (macaws, <u>sloths</u>, <u>butterflies</u>, monkeys)
3. The rainforest is being cut down for (space, <u>timber</u>, light)

Answer these questions.

4. How does the canopy protect the rainforest?
   The canopy provides a home for brightly coloured birds.
5. Write these layers of the rainforest in order, topmost one first:
   shrub layer, emergent layer, understory, forest floor, canopy.
   (1) *emergent layer* (2) *canopy* (3) *understory*
   (4) *shrub layer* (5) *forest floor*
6. What does 'fragile' in line 23 mean?
   Can brake eisily
7. What does 'displaced' in line 28 mean?
   Something isn't where it's spose to be.
8–9. Give two reasons why cutting down trees in the rainforest is damaging.
   because animals live there.
   because it's nature.

Underline a **noun** in each line.

10. pretty <u>book</u> went she busy
11. it large ready new <u>desk</u>
12. brown <u>Wednesday</u> ran some our
13. <u>legs</u> dirty them broken their
14. interesting <u>house</u> long dull her
15. from <u>Hannah</u> get old tipped
16. <u>paper</u> badly sad come too

Spell these words correctly. Each word has missing vowels.

17 y_o__u_ng   18 c_o__u_ntry
19 tr_o__u_bl_e_   20 t_o__u_ch
21 d_o__u_bl_e_

Add a sequence word at the beginning of each sentence so that it makes sense.

~~While~~   ~~After~~   ~~Then~~   ~~First~~

22–25 _First_ Tina sat in her chair while her teacher took the register. _Then_ she copied some sentences from the board. _While_ her teacher collected in the homework, Tina was writing. _After_ she had finished copying the sentences she was allowed out to play.

Circle the words that have two **syllables**.

26–31

fall   (bellow)   (arrow)   eel
(puppet)   (sparrow)   (wobble)
pill   tree   (pillow)

Rewrite the short passage, putting in the missing capital letters and full-stops.

32–40 mr scott visited edinburgh and glasgow each friday then he travelled on the overnight train to london

Mr Scott visited Edinburgh and Glasgow each Friday. Then he travelled on the overnight train to London.

Now go to the Progress Chart to record your score!   Total   40

Paper 2

When Eddie Dickens was eleven years old, both his parents caught some awful disease that made them turn yellow, go a bit crinkly around the edges, and smell of old hot-water bottles.

There were lots of diseases like that in those days. Perhaps it had something to do with all that thick fog, those knobbly cobbled streets and the fact that everyone went everywhere by horse … even to the bathroom. Who knows?

'It's very contagious,' said his father.

'And catching,' said his mother, sucking on an ice cube shaped like a famous general.

They were in Eddie's parents' bedroom, which was very dark and dingy and had no furniture in it except for a large double bed, an even larger wardrobe, and thirty-two different types of chair designed to make you sit up straight even if your wrists were handcuffed to your ankles.

'Why are you sucking an ice cube shaped like a famous general?' Eddie asked his parents, who were propped up against piles of pillows in their impressively ugly double bed.

'Doctor Muffin says that it helps with the swelling,' said his mother. In fact, because she had a famous-general-shaped ice cube in her mouth, what she actually said was, 'Dotter Muffin schez va it hewlpz wiva schwelln,' but Eddie managed to translate.

'What swelling?' he asked politely.

His mother shrugged, then suddenly looked even more yellow and even more crinkly round the edges.

'And why do they have to be famous-general-shaped?' asked Eddie. He always asked lots of questions and whenever he asked lots of questions his father would say: 'Questions! Questions!'

'Questions! Questions!' said his father.

Told you.

'But why a famous general?' Eddie repeated. 'Surely the shape of the ice cube can't make any difference?'

'Schows sow muck chew no,' muttered his mother, which meant (and still means), 'Shows how much you know.'

His father rustled the bedclothes. 'One does not question the good doctor,' he said. 'Especially when one is a child.' He was a small man except for when he was sitting up in bed. In this position, he looked extremely tall.

Then Eddie's mother rustled the bedclothes. It was easy to make them rustle because they were made entirely from brown paper bags glued together with those extra strips of gummed paper you sometimes get if you buy more than one stamp at the post office.

Postage stamps were a pretty new idea back then, and everyone – except for a great-great-great-aunt on my mother's side of the family – was excited about them.

From *A House Called Awful End* by Philip Ardagh

Underline the right answers.

1 Why did Eddie think there were lots of diseases 'in those days'?

(because it was cold, because people did not eat enough, because it was foggy)

2 Eddie's parents' bedroom had (no, a little, lots of) furniture in it.

3 Why had Doctor Muffin recommended chewing ice cubes?

(because they were cool, because they were easy to make, because they helped with a swelling)

Answer these questions.

4 What happened to Eddie's parents when he was eleven?

_____

5 What does 'contagious' mean in line 8?

_____

6 Why was it easy to rustle the bedclothes?

_____

7–8 List two details from the story that show that it was set a long time ago.

_____

_____

9 Say in your own words why you think this is going to be a rather strange story.

_____

Underline the two **antonyms** in each line.

10	right	back	left	correct
11	dark	light	day	winter
12	young	happy	dirty	clean
13	funny	rich	poor	ill
14	danger	safety	crash	freedom
15	here	now	then	where

Add the missing commas to these sentences.

16 Diane is making a blouse a skirt and a dress.

17–18 Steven bought some potatoes carrots cabbages and onions.

19–21 At school we study English mathematics history geography and art.

Add the **suffix** *ness* or *ment* to each of these words.

22 weak_____ 23 agree_____

24 pay_____ 25 enjoy_____

26 blind_____ 27 state_____

28 quiet_____ 29 ill_____

Underline an **adjective** that best describes the word in bold.

30	**station**	three	pink	heavy	busy
31	**pencil**	wet	sharp	sleepy	hot
32	**hands**	ten	happy	clean	first
33	**June**	sunny	foggy	dark	frosty
34	**hair**	sticky	sweet	quiet	straight

Match each word with its meaning. Write the number next to the word.

35 carrot	_____	(1) a funny picture
36 carpet	_____	(2) he makes things out of wood
37 carton	_____	(3) a vegetable
38 cartoon	_____	(4) a cardboard box
39 carol	_____	(5) floor covering
40 carpenter	_____	(6) a song

Now go to the Progress Chart to record your score!   Total   40

Paper 3

Scene 1

Mr Williams' classroom
Writing on blackboard – 'Mr Williams is a silly old fool'

Mark and Andy are playing in Mr Williams' classroom during playtime. They should have been outside. Suddenly they hear footsteps coming down the corridor.

Mark	Quick! Hide! He is coming, I can hear his footsteps.
Andy	Where? He has eyes in the back of his head. Even if we hide he will know we are here.
Mark	We must try – what about the store cupboard?

They both rush over to the store cupboard.

Footsteps getting closer.

Mark	It's locked.
Andy	Hurry up! Under Mr Williams' table.

Mark and Andy sitting under table.

Mark   I wish I hadn't written anything on the blackboard!

Sound of two sets of footsteps coming into the room.

Andy	*(whispering and peering under the desk)* It's not Mr Williams, it's a woman. I can see the legs. I think it's Mrs Wilkinson. She wears those shoes with the flat buckles. And there's someone else there. It looks like Miss Jones – black trousers, blue shoes with laces.
Mrs Wilkinson	*(to Miss Jones)* Now we're alone, Caroline, we can discuss the matter. *(suddenly catches sight of the board and laughs.)* He is too. Should have retired years ago, silly old fool. We'd better wipe it off though ... Anyway, as I was saying, what happened?
Miss Jones	Well, I left my handbag in the staff room and when I went back to look for it, the Head was coming out, very quickly, holding a large supermarket bag.
Mrs Wilkinson	Well, Caroline? So what?
Miss Jones	When I looked in the staff room, my handbag was gone.

Underline the right answers.

1 Which scene of the play is this?

(Scene 1, Scene 2, don't know)

2 Where did the boys first want to hide?

(behind a desk, under the teacher's table, in the store cupboard)

3 Miss Jones wore (flat shoes with a buckle, blue shoes with laces, trainers)

Answer these questions.

4 Why couldn't the boys hide in the cupboard?

_____

5 What was Miss Jones's first name?

_____

6 What made Mrs Wilkinson laugh?

_____

7 What was Miss Jones suggesting the Head might have done?

_____

8–9 What do you think happens next?

_____

_____

Circle the words that are spelt correctly.

10–13   enough   quater

exersise   naughty

oposite   important

interest   striaght   promise

Name the **collective noun** for each of the following.

14 twelve cows   _____

15 a large number of wasps   _____

16 a large area of trees   _____

17 a handful of flowers   _____

18 a group of sheep   _____

19 a side of football players   _____

Arrange these words in the order you would find them in the dictionary.

colour   dark   eel   dragon   egg   change

20 (1) _____   21 (2) _____   22 (3) _____

23 (4) _____   24 (5) _____   25 (6) _____

Underline the fronted adverbial in each of these sentences.

26 Before we leave, make sure you have been to the toilet.

27 The day after tomorrow, I'm going to Australia

28 Later that morning. I heard the school had flooded.

Write three sentences that begin with a fronted adverbial.

29 _____

30 _____

31 _____

Rewrite the **proper nouns** with capital letters.

swamp   birmingham   prince william   dexter
august   chester   block   monday   tap
abigail   mrs jones   magician   thursday

32 _____   33 _____   34 _____

35 _____   36 _____   37 _____

38 _____   39 _____   40 _____

Now go to the Progress Chart to record your score!   Total

Paper 4

Strange, strange, is the little old man
Who lives in the Grange.
Old, old, and they say that he keeps
A box full of gold.
Bowed, bowed, is his thin little back   5
Which once was so proud.
Soft, soft, are his steps as he climbs
The stairs to the loft.
Black, black, is the old shuttered house.
Does he sleep on a sack?   10
They say he does magic, that he can cast spells,
That he prowls round the garden listening for bells;
That he watches for strangers, hates every soul,
And peers with his dark eye through the keyhole.
I wonder, I wonder, as I lie in my bed,   15
Whether he sleeps with his hat on his head?
Is he really a magician with altar of stone
Or a lonely old gentleman left on his own?

Underline the right answers.

1 The man is (small, tall, medium height).

2 People say he keeps (jewels, gold, silver, pennies) in a box.

3 He walks upstairs (quietly, quickly, noisily).

Answer these questions.

4 What do people say he can do?

_____

5 What do people say he listens for?

_____

6 What is a 'loft'?

_____

7–8 Write two words that describe the man.

_____   _____

9 If the man is not a magician, what could he be?

_____

Add the correct **homophone** in each sentence.

10 **hear** or **here**   I can _____ the train coming.

11 **write** or **right**   Sam got all the answers _____.

12 **stares** or **stairs**   Grandpa climbed the _____ one at a time.

13 **saw** or **sore**   Kate _____ the horse galloping.

14 **road** or **rowed**   Tuhil and Frank _____ as fast as they could.

15 **Witch** or **Which**   _____ cake shall I have?

Underline the words that are spoken in these sentences.

16 "Quick, come here!" yelled the teacher.
17 "I'm waiting for my tea," answered Greg.
18 The children muttered, "Wish we didn't have to go to bed!"
19 "Shh, the baby is asleep," whispered Dad.
20 "You do look silly!" laughed Rupa.

Rewrite these sentences, making the **plurals singular**.

21 The trees swayed in the wind.

_____

22–23 The boys ate the sweets.

_____

24 The barking dogs scared the girl.

_____

25–27 Sophie collected the ponies and led them to the buckets of food.

_____

Make eight **compound words** out of the eleven short words.

card   worm   butter   man   cup   ball
snow   earth   post   egg   board

28 _____   **29** _____

30 _____   **31** _____

32 _____   **33** _____

34 _____   **35** _____

Write *am*, *is* or *are* in the sentence so that it makes sense.

36 They _____ going to the beach.

37 I _____ really going to miss you.

38 We _____ going to have a ride tomorrow.

39 David _____ very upset.

40 The twins _____ sharing a bedroom.

Paper 5

BIGVILLE WEEKLY ECHO
Homes facing the bulldozer
by Mike Smeaton

Heartbroken council tenants in the Nanton area of Bigville have little to celebrate over Christmas. They have just been told that their houses could be demolished because the council does not have the money to repair them.

The council recently surveyed 80 Westway type houses and found they were in very poor condition. They have severe structural problems and the repair bill has been put at 4.8 million.

Westway houses have steel frames and were built in large numbers to meet Britain's population growth in the 1950s. The houses were prefabricated in sections in the factory and bolted together on site. It was a quick and cheap solution to Britain's housing problem after the war. For speed, chemicals were used to harden the concrete. It was found in the 1980s that when exposed to water, the chemicals rotted the steel. Repairs were done in the 1990s to slow down the decay, but now the council thinks the damage is beyond repair. 'We simply don't have the funds to repair the houses any more,' said John Kennaway, the council engineer. 'Anyway it would be a very difficult task.'

Local residents are confused and angry. 'Quite honestly, it's made for a terrible Christmas,' said Jane Adams, who has lived in Ringway Close for 51 years. 'Many of us have lived here all our lives. I love my home and it's not just buildings that we're talking about. A whole community could be destroyed.'

Mrs Adams, who chairs the Residents' Association, said that the money should be found to preserve the houses. The council says it simply does not have the cash. Jeff Johnston, the councillor for housing, said there was no easy solution. Part of the problem is that the houses are semi-detached and some of them have been sold to private owners. If it wanted to bulldoze them, the council would have to buy back the privately owned houses first.

Underline the right answers.

1 Westway houses were built (before the war, during the war, after the war).

2 What is Jeff Johnston's job?

(councillor for housing, chair of the Residents' Association, council engineer)

3 Westway homes are (detached, bungalows, semi-detached).

Answer these questions.

4 What reason is given for Britain's housing problem after the war?

_____

5 Why were chemicals useful in building Westway houses?

_____

6 What does 'prefabricated' in line 19 mean?

_____

7 Write two words to describe how local residents feel about the problem.

(1) _____ (2) _____

8 Why doesn't Jane Adams want the houses destroyed?

_____

9–10 Give two reasons why the council cannot repair the houses.

(1) _____

(2) _____

11 Explain in your own words what Mrs Adams meant when she said 'A whole community could be destroyed' (lines 42–43).

_____

Spell each of these words correctly.

12 vien   13 thay

14 nieghbour   15 wiegh

16 obay   17 eghty-eight

Circle the **pronouns** in each sentence.

18–19 They thought he sang beautifully.

20–21 It was the best day he could remember.

22–23 He said she was very clever.

24–25 They screamed to make him hear.

Underline the **root word** in each of these words.

26 dislike **27** jumping **28** unkind

29 frighten **30** passed **31** altogether

Rewrite these two sentences, adding the missing punctuation and capital letters.

32–36 david was unsure what day it was was it thursday

_____

_____

Underline a **synonym** for the word in bold.

37 pointed	shiny	sharp	dull	sloping
38 circle	square	peg	round	oblong
39 nation	country	ribbon	food	strip
40 busy	lazy	hard	soft	active

Now go to the Progress Chart to record your score!   Total 40

Paper 6

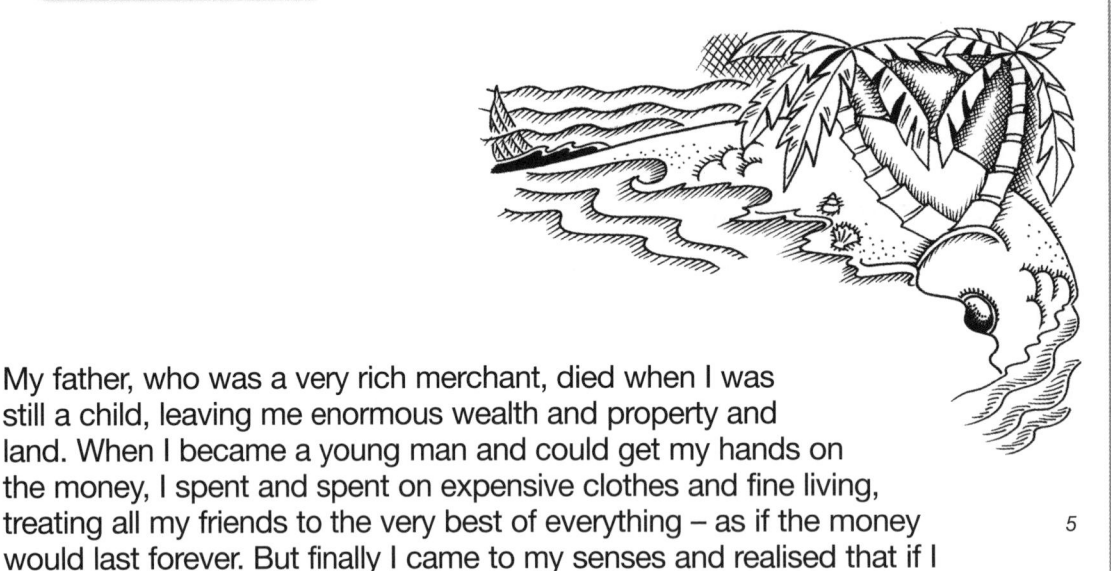

My father, who was a very rich merchant, died when I was
still a child, leaving me enormous wealth and property and
land. When I became a young man and could get my hands on
the money, I spent and spent on expensive clothes and fine living,
treating all my friends to the very best of everything – as if the money   5
would last forever. But finally I came to my senses and realised that if I
carried on in this way I should soon be facing poverty.

   So I resolved to do something about it. I sold my remaining
possessions and fine clothes for three thousand dirhams, enough to fund
me for a journey to foreign parts. And with the money I bought some   10
goods to trade with and all I needed for a long voyage, and joined a
company of merchants on board a vessel bound for Basra, where we
changed ship. We sailed for weeks on end, travelling through the Persian
Gulf and into the Arabian Sea, going from island to island, until finally we
reached an island that looked just like the gardens of Paradise.   15

   We cast anchor and landed, and in no time we were busying ourselves
in our different ways: making ovens in the sand, cooking, washing,
exploring, and playing games to amuse ourselves. At one point I thought
I felt a small earth tremor, but nobody else seemed to notice it. They just
carried on with what they were doing. I went off with a small group to   20
explore, but we hadn't ventured very far before we heard the ship's
captain hailing us from the gunwale at the top of his voice.

   'Run for your lives!' he was calling. 'Drop everything and get back on
board. This isn't an island, after all. We've landed on a monstrous fish
that's been asleep so long that the sands have settled over it and the   25
trees have sprung up on it. But when you lit your fires it felt the heat and
began to stir. At any moment it will plunge down into the depths, taking
you all with it. Get back to the ship before you drown!'

   We didn't need any persuading, I can tell you. We abandoned our
bundles of merchandise, our spare clothes, our cooking pots, and   30
everything else in our mad scramble back to the ship.

From *The Seven Voyages of Sinbad the Sailor* by John Yeoman

Underline the right answers.

1 The father of the person in the story had been a (sailor, merchant, soldier, fisherman).

2 Which of these seas did the ship sail to?

(the Indian Ocean, the Black Sea, the Arabian Sea, the Pacific Ocean, the Persian Gulf)

3 The fish woke up because of (an earth tremor, the shouting of the men, the fires).

Answer these questions.

4 Say in your own words why the person in the story needed to change his life.

_____

5 What does 'resolved' mean in line 8?

_____

6 Why did the passengers and crew not notice they had landed on a fish?

_____

7 What warning did the person telling the story have that there was something strange about the island?

_____

8 How do you think the people felt when they discovered that they weren't on an island?

_____

Add the **prefix** or **suffix** *al* to each of these words.

9 _____ways_____   10 _____historic_____   11 _____so_____

12 _____ready_____   13 _____mechanic_____   14 _____medic_____

15 _____accident_____ 16 _____though_____   17 _____most_____

Write each of these verbs in the **past tense**.

18 walk _____   **19** jump _____

20 pull _____   **21** sprint _____

22 push _____   **23** listen _____

Put one of the **conjunctions** in each of the spaces below.

until   but   because   so

24 Marianne stayed at home _____ she had a cold.

25 The sea is quite warm _____ we can go swimming.

26 Mum is going out now _____ she will be back soon.

27 'Don't eat the biscuit _____ you've finished your lunch.'

28 We will stay here _____ dad asked us to.

Write the *nch* or *tch* word to match each picture.

29 l_____   **30** i_____   **31** s_____

32 b_____   **33** p_____   **34** s_____

Using a line, match each word with its correct **definition**.

35 voyage   every year
36 remedy   a long journey
37 summit   a piece broken off something
38 annual   a large, deep spoon
39 ladle   a cure
40 fragment   the top

Paper 7

Rosie hurried on. The pubs were further apart now and even the alleys were silent. Just the odd moggie, poor things, scavenging at the pigswill bins.

She was just bending down to stroke one when the siren went. For the third time that day. Rosie got the usual sinking feeling in her gut, but she wasn't all that worried. Air-raid sirens couldn't kill you. She listened intently, through the dying drone of the siren, for the sound of bombers' engines…

And heard nothing.

She'd carry on for a bit, try and get home before anything happened. Her ma would worry if she was caught out in a raid. Ma might even leave the shelter and come looking for her, as far as the chippie in Scobie Street. Then batter Rosie over the ear when she found her, for causing so much worry.

'G'night, moggie. Best of British Luck!'

Her footsteps quickened; the gas mask banged harder against her bottom, as if urging her on.

She'd gone nearly half a mile before she heard the bombers coming. She was in a district she hardly knew. Really poor people, to judge from the state of their doors and windows. But you couldn't be choosy when the bombers came. You just ran for the nearest brick street-shelter with its concrete-slab roof.

Not many shelters round here. Poor people were always the worst looked after. Bet the toffs had shelters, and to spare, up Croxteth way…

She ran and ran. Turned a corner by a chapel with bombed-out windows. Saw the three brass balls of a pawnbroker's… Then a great square shelter loomed up.

She made the doorway, just as the first guns opened up overhead, turning the night white-black, white-black. Making a noise like some daft kid banging a tin tray right in your ear that echoed across the whole sky after.

Then she heard the shrapnel shrieking down like dead rockets on
Bonfire Night. And ducked through the blackout curtain into the shelter.
   There was room by the door, on the slatted benches… She flung
herself into it, to get her breath back…
   Still panting, she looked around. 35
   And sighed. It seemed a totally miserable sort of shelter.
   People huddled together in a dim blue light. Silent except for the
racking cough and the dismal wail of a baby at the far end.

From *Blitz* by Robert Westall

Underline the right answers.

1 What was Rosie doing when the siren went?

   (looking for shelter, looking in pigswill bins, stroking a moggie)

2 She was carrying (a suitcase, a gas mask, an umbrella).

3 The guns sounded like (dead rockets, a tray being banged, the sea hitting cliffs).

Answer these questions.

4 How did Rosie feel when she heard the sirens?

5 Why did Rosie think that her mother might hit her round the head?

6 How could Rosie tell that she had come to a poor area?

7 Who do you think the 'toffs' are in line 24?

8 Describe in your own words what made the shelter seem so miserable.

Put these words in the **past tense**.

9 go _____

10 sing _____

11 jump _____

12 fight _____

13 buy _____

14 come _____

Rewrite these sentences using a more interesting phrase than the words in bold.

15 We had a good time at the **party**.

_____

16 My **teacher** is very grumpy.

_____

17 Daniel climbed out of the **pool** and got dressed.

_____

18 The **baby** screamed until it was picked up.

_____

19 The **children** had a fun day.

_____

20 Joseph was reading a **book**.

_____

Add the ly suffix to each of these words.

21 grumpy _____   **22** poor   _____

23 sad   _____   **24** quick _____

25 kind   _____   **26** happy _____

27 stupid   _____   **28** rough _____

Many railway lines link London with other parts of the country. There are two main lines to Scotland: one goes up the east side of the country through York and Newcastle, and the other goes up the west side, passing through Crewe and Carlisle. If you are travelling to North Wales you leave the main line at Crewe. There are fast trains from Liverpool, Manchester and Sheffield to London and it is much easier to travel from north to south than it is to travel from east to west. There is a fast service from London to the West Country which passes through Salisbury and Exeter. There is an excellent electric service between London and south-east England.

Underline the right answers.

29–30 Which two of these towns would you pass through if you were travelling from London to Scotland on the east side of the country?
(Crewe, York, Salisbury, Manchester, Carlisle, Newcastle)

31 Which direction is it easier to travel in?
(east to west, north to south)

Answer these questions.

32 If you were travelling to North Wales, where do you leave the main line?

_____

33–34 Name two cities that have fast trains to London.

_____   _____

35 What is the service like between London and south-east England?

_____

Add the missing commas to these sentences where a short pause or pauses are needed.

36–37 Harry a very nervous boy hated the thunderstorm.

38 The boys set off along the track anxious to get to the next village before dark.

39 Najib ran as fast as he could barely taking a breath.

40 Leena was starving having not had anything to eat all day.

Now go to the Progress Chart to record your score!   Total   40

Paper 8

Zanzibar

Zanzibar used to make me think
Of marzipan and stripes.
It has the sounds of bees in it, and zizz.

I didn't know it would smell of spice
of lemon grass and strips of cinnamon   5
green balls of pepper,

buds of cloves,
nutmeg and vanilla pods
and rain, and steamy rain.

Children cling beneath banana leaves   10
and splash home, laughing, through the mud.
Soon the rain will wash their homes away.

Their mothers watch the sky.
When the sun dries the earth
They will squat and scoop and daub   15
and build their huts again.

Zanzibar. Palm trees and red skies
Blue fireflies in the night
Cinnamon, cloves, and lemon grass, and rain.

by Berlie Doherty

Underline the right answers.

1 Zanzibar is (a colour, a smell, a sound, a place).

2 Which of these smells does the poet not mention?

(vanilla, cinnamon, nutmeg, ginger, cloves)

3 At night in the poem you can see (stars, fireflies, the moon, the sea).

Answer these questions.

4 Find something that is green in the poem and something that is red.

_____

5 What is the weather like in Zanzibar?

_____

6 Why do the mothers need to watch the skies in Zanzibar?

_____

7 Why might the sound of the word 'Zanzibar' remind the author of the sound of bees?

_____

8 Do you think that the poet has been to Zanzibar? Use evidence from the poem to support your answer.

_____

Write the missing **noun** with an apostrophe to show something belongs to someone.

9 The rabbit belonged to Dimitri. It was _____ rabbit.

10 The crayons belonged to Jane. They were _____ crayons.

11 The jacket belonged to Helen. It was _____ jacket.

12 The bone belonged to Mop the dog. It was _____ bone.

13 The rat belonged to Rajeeh. It was _____ rat.

14 The books belonged to Soraya. They were _____ books.

Write each of these words correctly. A letter in each word needs to be changed to a y.

15 mith _____   **16** gim _____

17 Egipt _____   **18** mistery _____

19 piramid _____

Circle the **nouns** that don't have a different **plural** form.

20–23   reindeer   gate   grapefruit   jacket
             goldfish   fork   sheep   button

Underline a **synonym** for the word in bold.

24	**aid**	act	hinder	help	stop
25	**drop**	rain	prod	bounce	fall
26	**sad**	strict	unhappy	glad	ugly
27	**quick**	loud	fast	slow	quiet
28	**several**	few	both	some	none
29	**enjoy**	hate	like	suffer	drive
30	**modern**	new	old	ancient	great
31	**depart**	post	leave	come	send

Write the **plural** of each of these **nouns** ending in *f*.

32 hoof _____   33 shelf _____

34 loaf _____   35 calf   _____

36 leaf _____   37 wolf   _____

Write an interesting sentence about each of the following.

38 your home

_____

39 your hair

_____

40 your teacher

_____

Now go to the Progress Chart to record your score!   Total   40

Paper 9

How to make a Christmas pudding

You need:

1 cup plain flour

1 tablespoon mixed spice

$\frac{2}{3}$ cup brown sugar

3 cups mixed dried fruit

A pinch of salt

1 cup shredded suet

1 large egg, beaten

$\frac{1}{2}$ cup brown ale

Butter or margarine to grease the basin

1. Get a large mixing bowl. Mix everything in the bowl except the egg and the ale.
2. Add the egg and the ale. Stir them in. Put the mixture in a cool place and cover with a cloth. Leave for a day.
3. Grease a 900 ml/1.5 pint pudding basin. Cut out a circle of non-stick baking paper and line the bottom of the basin.
4. Stir the pudding again and tip it into the basin. Cover with a circle of greaseproof paper. Put an old saucer over the top. Then cover it with a double thickness of foil. Fold it over the edge of the basin all the way round. Tie string round to hold it on tight over the basin.
5. Put the basin into a steamer over a pan of boiling water. Cover with a lid. Steam the pudding for 6 hours. **Caution: you must check the steamer every half an hour to make sure there is enough boiling water in the pan. Top it up as needed.**
6. Re-cover the pudding. Store it in a cool place. Steam it for another 2.5 hours before serving it. Happy Christmas!

Write true or false by each of these statements.

1. You must have brandy to go in the pudding. _____
2. You put the butter or margarine into the mixture. _____
3. You need a rolling pin to make the pudding. _____
4. You need to beat the egg before you put it in. _____
5. You need to line the basin before you pour the mixture in. _____
6. Putting a string round the pudding basin helps to carry it. _____
7. You can make a Christmas pudding in a day. _____

Answer this question.

8 What do you think will happen if you do not check the steamer every half an hour while the pudding is cooking?

_____

Write a more powerful **verb** for each of the verbs in bold.

9 Harry **walked** to Gary's house. _____

10 "May I have a cake?" **said** Meena. _____

11 Dave **took** his pen back from Ann. _____

12 "Please can I watch television?" **said** Nigel. _____

13 The man **ran** round the park. _____

Put these words correctly into the table.

chef   echo
    character
      machine
scheme   brochure

14–19

| words with... ||
ch sounding 'sh' as in shout	ch sounding 'c' as in cat

The following sentences are not in the right order. Read them through carefully, and then write the numbers to show their correct order.

20 _____ (1) The cyclist lay on the road.

21 _____ (2) Then the policeman called for an ambulance.

22 _____ (3) A cyclist was knocked off his bicycle.

23 _____ (4) Finally the cyclist was taken to hospital.

24 _____ (5) Meanwhile a policeman arrived.

25 _____ (6) Next the ambulance arrived.

With a line, join each word with its **diminutive** (word implying smallness).

26 owl   duckling
27 cat   piglet
28 goose   owlet
29 pig   bullock
30 duck   kitten
31 bull   gosling

Rewrite the sentences, adding in the missing punctuation and capital letters.

32–35 the plane landed at heathrow airport a little late

_____

36–40 tessa and claire admitted they were lost what were they going to do

_____

Now go to the Progress Chart to record your score!   Total   40

Paper 10

Stopping by Woods on a Snowy Evening

Whose woods these are I think I know.
His house is in the village, though;
He will not see me stopping here
To watch his woods fill up with snow.

My little horse must think it queer   5
To stop without a farmhouse near
Between the woods and frozen lake
The darkest evening of the year.

He gives his harness bells a shake
To ask if there is some mistake.   10
The only other sound's the sweep
Of easy wind and downy flake.

The woods are lovely, dark, and deep,
But I have promises to keep,
And miles to go before I sleep,   15
And miles to go before I sleep.

by Robert Frost

Underline the right answers.

1 At what time of day is this poem set?
(morning, afternoon, evening)

2 Where does the owner of the woods live?
(in a farmhouse, in the woods, in a village)

3 Where does the rider stop his horse?
(in the woods, beside the woods, a long way from the woods)

Answer these questions.

4–5 Describe two sounds the rider can hear.

(1) _____

(2) _____

6 Why would the rider's horse think it 'queer' to stop where they have?

_____

7 Which line in the poem tells you that the rider loves the woods, rather than is frightened of them?

_____

8 How do you think you would feel about the woods if you were making the same journey? Why?

_____

Write the word or words each of these **contractions** is made from.

9 should've _____ 10 won't _____

11 I'll _____ 12 can't _____

13 they've _____ 14 isn't _____

15 wouldn't _____ 16 haven't _____

Add the missing speech marks to these sentences.

17 Have you found the dog? asked Jim.

18 Let's go and play in the park, suggested Aman.

19 I don't think you have washed your face! joked Dad.

20 Are you enjoying the pizza? asked the waitress.

21 I wish it would stop raining, sighed Amy.

22 Where do you think you are going? asked Mrs Thrower.

Rewrite the word adding the **suffix** *ible* or *able*. (Remember, if the last letter of the word is a vowel, the last letter is usually dropped before adding the suffix.)

23 suit _____

24 reason _____

25 sense _____

26 believe _____

27 wash _____

28 response _____

Underline the **adverbs** in these sentences.

29 The old man shouted angrily at the children.

30 The child ran noisily along the corridor.

31 The cat slowly stretched her leg.

32 Billy neatly wrote the date at the top of the page.

33 The robin sang sweetly as the snow fell.

34 My Dad snored loudly in front of the television.

With a line, match a word in each column to make a **compound word**. Write the compound words.

over	room	35	_____
moon	fall	36	_____
some	head	37	_____
water	light	38	_____
drain	where	39	_____
class	pipe	40	_____

Now go to the Progress Chart to record your score! Total 40

Paper 11

A Visitor's Guide to Athens

Athens is one of the oldest of all cities. Named after Athena, the Greek goddess of wisdom, its history stretches back over 3000 years. It is home to one of the world's most famous buildings. The white marble temple, the Parthenon, sits on a hill right in the centre of the city. It can be seen for miles around. It took about eight years to build and was completed in 438 BC. It is one of the main reasons why tourists visit Athens.

However, when visitors come to modern Athens for the first time they are rather surprised by what they find. Athens is very big. About 4 million people live there. It is a lively, modern, busy place with many urban problems. There are huge traffic jams in the city's streets and considerable air pollution. Sometimes the smog is so thick that it is almost impossible to see the Parthenon on its hill. Acid rain is eating away at the marble of the ancient buildings and has already caused irreversible damage.

Fortunately in the last few years there have been some improvements in the air quality. In preparation for the Olympic Games, which were staged in Athens in 2004, the city built a new metro system. The rail network carries 400,000 passengers a day. It is estimated to have removed 200,000 cars from the streets. For the Games Athens also built a wonderful new airport on the edge of the city.

Athens has very hot summers. In July and August the average daytime temperature is 31°C. Athenians tend to stay out late at night when it's cooler. No one eats much before 9 pm, and many shows and entertainments don't start until midnight. You need to be able to stay up late in Athens! Winters, on the other hand, can be quite cold and the city has snowfalls most years. The best times to come are spring and autumn – and there's lots to do: museums, art galleries, restaurants and nightlife. And if you get tired of it all, take the metro to the city's port and hop on a boat to one of the hundreds of Greek islands where you can lie in the sun and get away from the crowds.

Underline the right answers.

1. When was the Parthenon built?
   (by 438 BC, 3000 years ago, we don't know)
2. The ancient buildings are damaged by (tourists, earthquakes, acid rain).
3. The climate in Athens is (wet, warm all the year round, hot in summer).

Answer these questions.

4–5 List two things that surprise visitors to Athens.

That it was really big.

that the air was polouted.

6 Why is acid rain so damaging?

Sokes into the marbell

7 What benefits did the 2004 Olympic Games bring to Athens?

metro system, an airport.

8 Explain why you would or would not like to visit Athens, using information from the visitor's guide.

I would like to go, too see the parthenon.

Underline all the **proper nouns**.

9–16 ten   Thursday   River Thames   cat   Kate   lunch
      Queen Elizabeth   tonight   Jake   Mr Norton
         September   line   London

Write two sentences for each **homonym**. In each sentence the homonym must have a different meaning.

17–18 fly

(1) A fly is an insect.
(2) Planes can fly.

19–20 match

(1) I light the fire with a Match.
(2) England won the football match.

21–22 chest

(1) I have a chest full of treasure.
(2) My chest is underneath my chin.

Add *its* or *it's* to fill the gap in each sentence. Don't forget to use a capital letter where necessary.

23 The cat jumped out of __Its__ bed.

24 "__It's__ time we went to school," called Mum.

25 The elephant drank through __its__ trunk.

26 "__It's__ Sophie at the door, Amy," Dad shouted.

27–28 "__It's__ autumn and time the tree lost __its__ leaves," commented Nathan.

Find eight words in the wordsearch ending in *ild* or *ind*.

b	c	h	i	l	d	t
l	g	k	n	d	s	a
i	g	o	w	t	j	f
n	r	f	i	i	h	i
d	m	i	l	d	n	n
k	i	n	d	s	e	d
s	b	e	h	i	n	d

29–36 child   wild   mild   wind
behind   blind   kind   find

Add the missing **consonant letters** to each word to make a wild animal.

37 e l e p h a n t
38 L i o n
39 e m u
40 g i r a f f e

Paper 12

Mia is being bullied at school by a gang called the C.I.S.

On Saturday morning they woke me up at a quarter past seven.

Their text message was short and not at all sweet.

PAY UP ON MON OR ELSE

After seeing that I couldn't stop shaking. In the end I put the blankets over my head and curled up tightly into a ball.

Oh how I hated their messages. Hated them, hated them, HATED THEM. In fact, I nearly got up and threw my mobile out of the window. Then I stopped myself, because that would have been a daft thing to do – and anyway, they'd just love me to do that.

So instead I lay under my covers worrying about Monday … What were we going to do? We'd joked about handing them fake money or giving them the five pounds all in two-pence pieces. But I was pretty certain we'd hand over the money. It seemed the easiest and safest option – for now.

I had just one problem with that. I was flat broke.

I'd insisted on paying Oliver back the four pounds he'd loaned me. And the rest – which wasn't much – I'd spent on sweets and a magazine.

Of course, I could ask Oliver to lend me another five pounds. And I knew he would. But that just seemed to be taking advantage of his good nature. What else could I do? Well, I could always try and explain to the C.I.S. that I only get twelve pounds a month pocket money. And remind them again that my dad was out of work for a year.

It would all just be a waste of my breath, though. Chris Freyer would enjoy seeing me grovel to her. But she wouldn't understand. That chip on her shoulder was so huge it blotted out everything else. So it seemed I had no choice but to put out the begging bowl to my parents.

My dad was home now, but he was not in the best of moods. I think he was just dead tired with his new job and all the training he'd just done, but he was kind of irritable and impatient. Then, in the afternoon he took my two little brothers swimming: this was the moment to work on my mum.

To butter her up I offered to do the hoovering downstairs. I did it extra thoroughly too.

From *Traitor* by Pete Johnson

Underline the right answers.

1. The gang told Mia to pay on (Monday, Tuesday, Wednesday, Thursday).
2. She decided (not to pay, to give them fake money, only to pay in two-pence pieces, to pay properly).
3. For pocket money she got (four, five, twelve) pounds a month.

Answer these questions.

4. Why couldn't Mia stop shaking?

   _____

5. What did Mia nearly do?

   _____

6. Why was it hard to ask her dad for money?

   _____

7. Explain in your own words why it was a waste of time explaining to the gang that she could not pay.

   _____

8. Why did Mia do the hoovering extra thoroughly?

   _____

9. What would you do if you were being asked for money?

   _____

Underline the correct **homophone** in the brackets.

10. I have never (seen, scene) so many people there.
11. The (bough, bow) of the tree had broken off.
12. The man gave the queen a graceful (bough, bow).
13. There was a big (hole, whole) in the ground.
14. The (hole, whole) school went to see the play.
15. The dog ate the (meet, meat) in his bowl.
16. Jess said she'd (meet, meat) Callum at the park.

Write the following lines in a shortened form, using the apostrophe.

Example: the glove belonging to the lady   *the lady's glove*

17 the jeans worn by the girl   _____

18 the shoe belonging to my father   _____

19 the toy the child had   _____

20 the paw of the dog   _____

21 the pencil Ravi owned   _____

22 the bracelet belonging to my gran   _____

Add sure or ture to these letters to make a word.

23 trea_____   24 pic_____

25 adven_____   26 mea_____

27 enclo_____   28 crea_____

Underline the **adjectives** in each sentence.

29 The shaggy dog panted loudly.

30–31 Tom's bright blue coat suited him well.

32 The glistening raindrops hung on the branches.

33 Naomi slept in her cosy bed.

34–35 Donna's long, golden hair had all been cut off!

Write a more powerful **verb** for each of these verbs.

Example: take   grab

36 say   _____   37 look   _____

38 walk _____   39 call   _____

40 touch _____

Now go to the Progress Chart to record your score!   Total   40

Paper 13

This story is set in Victorian London. Jamie and his friends make a living hunting for scraps beside the Thames.

Low tide was early next morning.

I'm a mudlark. I make my money by picking up the coal that falls out when they're unloading the brigs. I have a little basket strapped to my back. Sometimes I fill it twice in a day. Not that often, though.

I'm a good worker. I go out mudlarking even in the winter when most of the others can't stand the cold. It was only me and Davies and Ten Tons and maybe Patty and a couple of others by Blackwall pier this winter. Ten Tons and me are fine with it, but Davies turns blue with cold. I'm tougher than Davies, even though he's stronger than me. I can work all day even in the winter, when you have to crack the ice to lever the coals out of the mud. It's all Davies can do to sit on the bank and shiver and cry because his hands and feet hurt so much.

Sometimes the coal lies on the surface of the mud, but often it sinks under. Then you have to feel in the thick mud with your toes and hands. It's exciting when you find a big piece, but it's usually little nibs. When the basket's full I take it and sell my coal to the old women up and down Cotton Street or around All Saint's.

We don't just pick up coals, we pick up anything that gets dropped, just about. You get a farthing a pound for old iron. You get ha'pence for bits of rope. If you find fat the cooks have dropped overboard you can get three farthings for that. For good new copper, you can get up to four pence a pound.

Most things can be sold in this world. Once I made a shilling in a day. Mostly it's more like seven or eight pence.

From *The Copper Treasure* by Melvin Burgess

Underline the right answers.

1. What word is used to describe what the children in the story do?

   (treasure hunting, mudlarking, scavenging)

2. What are they looking to find in the river?

   (coal, gold, rubber)

3 What was the most Jamie ever made in a day? (four pence, a shilling, seven pence, eight pence).

Answer these questions.

4 Write in your own words why low tide was important to Jamie.
___

5 What is a 'brig' (line 3)?
___

6 Why did Davies find it so hard to work in winter?
___

7 What excited Jamie when he was out mudlarking?
___

8 Who bought the coal from Jamie?
___

9 Explain in your own words why mudlarking was so hard.
___

Write this sentence again, adding the missing punctuation and capital letters.
10–15 as Wendy headed to the door she called have you seen my hat
___
___

Add the missing apostrophes to these **plural nouns**.
Example: the six boys books   the six boys' books

16 the three dogs collars ___

17 the five girls socks ___

18 the nine hens eggs ___

19 the two cats bowls ___

20 the four dolls beds ___

21 the five boys footballs _____

22 the three spiders webs _____

Next to each **verb** write two **adverbs** that could describe it.

23–24 walk _____ _____

25–26 sleep _____ _____

27–28 eat _____ _____

29–30 draw _____ _____

31–35 Match the words with the same spelling patterns using a line.

antique	echo
league	reign
through	unique
chorus	thought
vein	tongue

Underline a **synonym** for the word in bold.

36 **fell**	dropped	flew	rose	felt
37 **rush**	blow	bump	knock	hurry
38 **unlike**	different	same	unkind	similar
39 **beneath**	above	beyond	away	under
40 **choose**	like	eat	select	present

Now go to the Progress Chart to record your score!   Total   40

Paper 14

Vote for Ben Barton!

Just writing to let you know it's time to choose the Form Captain again. Yes, I know it's a dreadful bore thinking about it, but to save your tiny brains the effort, I've got a dead simple solution – vote for me, Ben Barton, the number one choice for Form Five.

Why? Easy! Who came top of exams last year? Who's the leading goal scorer in the school team? Who knows how to calm Mr Wilkinson down when he's in a mood? Who hid Mrs Tollbart's specs so she couldn't mark our homework last week? Who will represent you best at the school council, as long as you pay me (just joking!)? Who can do juggling tricks with the bean bags?

And just think what the alternatives are! Sally Hunt – the biggest airhead in the class? Dwayne 'the Gorilla' Smith? I don't think so. Denzil Steel-Perkins? With a name like that he'd better stay class librarian. There's really only one choice – me! So vote, vote, vote for Brainy Ben, I say!

Dear Fellow Class Members

I'm writing to ask for your vote in the elections for Form Captain. I realise it's hard to decide who to vote for. It's easy to choose your best friend, or the person who shouts loudest, but it's best to choose someone who will help the whole class. I'd like to give you five reasons for considering me.

1. I kept the class library in perfect shape last year so that we won the Tidy Books competition.
2. I saved Izzy from eating himself to death when someone (whose initials begin with BB) put too much food in his water tank.
3. I lent everyone in the class my Supertronics DVD last term, though I'm still waiting for it back from The Person Who Overfed Izzy.
4. I will campaign for an extra five minutes at break time.
5. I have already asked Mr Wilkinson if we can have afterschool footie and netball.

Whoever you vote for, I'll still be your friend.

Best wishes

Denzil

Underline the right answers.

1. Which of these things can Ben not do?
   (play football, juggle, feed Izzy properly, calm down Mr Wilkinson)
2. The form captain has to:
   (tidy the library, feed Izzy, represent the class at the school council, juggle beanbags).
3. Who was called 'the Gorilla'?
   (Sally, Denzil, Dwayne, Izzy, Ben)

Answer these questions.

4. Who or what is Izzy?

   _____

5. List something each boy has already done to help the class.

   Ben _____

   Denzil _____

6. Explain in your own words why Denzil might not like Ben.

   _____

7. Whose letter is more persuasive? Give reasons for your choice.

   _____

Write each of these **nouns** in their **plural** form.

8. banana _____
9. fox _____
10. lorry _____
11. tray _____
12. church _____
13. brush _____
14. girl _____
15. beach _____

Add the missing comma to each of these sentences.

16. First thing this morning we met for a swim with our new friends.
17. Later that day Daniel's gran did a magic trick.
18. Although her face didn't show it she was very unhappy.
19. Her eyes drowsy with sleep Fran dozed off.
20. Looking for his home the dog ran on ahead.
21. Groping in the dark Sam found the light switch.

Underline the feminine word for the word in bold.

22 **prince**	fairy	woman	princess	queen
23 **duke**	player	actress	lady	duchess
24 **husband**	mother	father	wife	aunt
25 **uncle**	nephew	aunt	niece	sister
26 **he**	her	him	them	she
27 **nephew**	uncle	niece	cousin	woman
28 **brother**	sister	mother	child	twin

Underline the **adjectival phrase** in each sentence.

29 The large, brown clock hung on the wall.
30 The bright, loud, flashing fireworks exploded in the air.
31 Sam, the long-haired, shaggy dog, loved going for a walk.
32 The stern, pale-faced teacher glared at the children.
33 Caroline's coat, soaked and muddy, didn't look new any more.
34 Rain poured from the grey, heavy clouds.

Use each of these **pronouns** in a sentence.

35 I

_____

36 ours

_____

37 him

_____

38 mine

_____

39 they

_____

40 she

_____

Paper 15

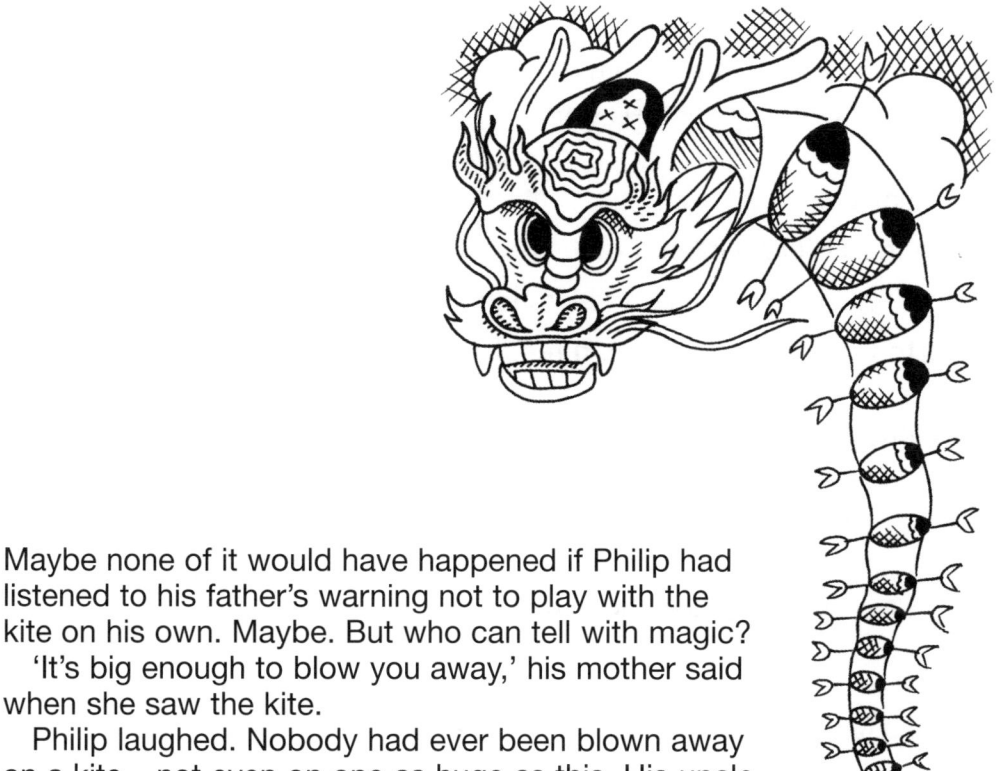

Maybe none of it would have happened if Philip had listened to his father's warning not to play with the kite on his own. Maybe. But who can tell with magic?

'It's big enough to blow you away,' his mother said when she saw the kite.

Philip laughed. Nobody had ever been blown away on a kite – not even on one as huge as this. His uncle had brought it back as a present from China and it really was the biggest and best you'd ever seen. It was shaped like a dragon and was coloured red, yellow and green.

Philip wanted to go out and fly it at once but his father said he had to wait until the weekend. The weekend! That was a whole four days away.

Philip put the kite in the corner of his bedroom. Every time he looked at it, he heard a voice whispering in his head.

'Go on,' the voice said, 'it's your kite. Dad's just a spoil-sport. Go on – it'll be good fun. No one will know if you sneak out for half an hour.'

For two days Philip managed to say 'no' to the voice, but on the third day he gave in …

The kite was so big that his arms ached from holding it up so that it didn't touch the ground. It was so big that by the time he reached the top of the hill in the park he was out of breath …

He looked up. A small, round, black cloud was racing across the blue sky. It was moving faster than any cloud Philip had ever seen. He felt the kite move in his hand. The long dragon's tail wagged from side to side like a dog's when it sees a friend.

The cloud got nearer and nearer the sun. Philip saw its shadow come racing up the hill towards him. It grew darker and Philip waited for the shadow to pass. But when he looked up, the cloud had stopped, directly in front of the sun. Its shadow formed a perfect circle all around him.

Then, out of nowhere came the wind. Whistling and spinning and howling. Philip closed his eyes. He felt his arms rise up above him as the wind caught the kite and lifted it. For a moment, he thought of letting go but there was a sudden tug and it was too late.

From *Beaver Towers* by Nigel Hinton

Underline the right answers.

1 The kite came from (Peru, China, France, America).

2 Philip kept the kite in (the garage, the kitchen, his bedroom).

3 Philip gave in to the voice after (four, three, two, five) days.

Answer these questions.

4 What did the voice try to make Philip think about his father?

_____

5 How did Philip feel as he carried the kite to the park?

_____

6–7 What two things were very unusual about the cloud's behaviour?

(1) _____

(2) _____

8 What, in the story, tells you that there was a connection between the kite and the cloud?

_____

Circle words that are **nouns**.

9–16   gatepost   happy   bunch   laughed
       Wednesday   greasy   sadly   Tom
       Edinburgh   Edward   freedom
       stream   famous   fought

Rewrite these sentences, adding the missing speech marks.

17 Come quickly! screamed Sam.

_____

18 How are you, Gran? asked Peter.

_____

19 It's time to go, sighed Mum.

_____

20 This way to the Tunnel of Screams, directed the attendant.

_____

21 Have we got time? enquired Nancy.

_____

22 Where are my slippers? exclaimed Grandad.

_____

Choose the most suitable **adverb** from the words below to put in each space. Each word may only be used once.

cheerfully   then   gently   here   loudly

23 The soldier stood _____, guarding the palace.

24 The nurse removed the dressing _____.

25 The ducks in the pond quacked _____.

26 The old man _____ greeted his friend.

27 The boys pushed past her _____ ran off laughing.

Add the **suffix** *ion* to each word, but be careful as some letters may need to be removed or added.

Example: explode + ion = explosion

28 express + ion = _____

29 inform + ion = _____

30 discuss + ion = _____

31 extend + ion = _____

32 educate + ion = _____

33 pollute + ion = _____

6

Write an **antonym** of each word.

34 happy _____

35 large _____

36 catch _____

37 noisy _____

38 thin _____

39 above _____

40 down _____

7

Now go to the Progress Chart to record your score! Total 40

Paper 16

Dear Gail

As you live near me in Denton, here are directions for getting to my party on foot:

* Go out of your gate. Turn left. Go to the end of Shelborn Avenue. Turn right into River Road. Go as far as the post-box. Cross the road there. (Be careful. Cars come fast up the road.) Go down the footpath opposite, past the horse field. (Usually two old ponies in there, very keen on carrots!)

* At the end you're in Harbour Road. Don't take the right to the sea front. Turn left, go past St James Church with the spire, cross the road again, take the third right into Oaktree Road. (There's a house with a red gate just before the turn.) Go about 90 metres until you see a sign on the right hand side that says 'Public Footpath, no bicycles'. Don't take this. Just beyond there's another path between two very tall houses. It's not marked at all.

* Go down there, over the footbridge. When you get to the end, you're in our road, Mill Road. It's a very long road, so you've still got a way to go.

* Turn left. Keep going until you see the second church, St John's, on the right, with a tower. Our house is seven beyond that, number 58. It's got a holly hedge and balloons outside.

* It should take you about 20 minutes. Any problems just ring on your mobile. Our number is 552961.

See you there!

Imran

P.S. I'm sure everyone in Denton will think you wearing a pirate hat in public is quite normal!

Underline the right answers.

1 Gail lives in (Harbour Road, Mill Road, Shelborn Avenue, River Road).
2 Gail lives near (a motorway, the sea, a supermarket).
3 St John's church has (a tower, a spire, a flag).
4 Mill Road is (long, dangerous, straight).

Answer these questions.

5 Write down these roads in the order that Gail will travel along them:

Oaktree, River, Harbour, Mill, Shelborn.

(1) _____ (2) _____ (3) _____

(4) _____ (5) _____

6 Where would you go to post a letter?

_____

7 What can't you do on the footpath in Oaktree Road?

_____

8 What address does Imran live at? Include the name of the town.

_____

9 What was the fancy dress theme for the party?

_____

Put one of the **conjunctions** in each of the spaces below.

but   although   than   and   if   so

10 He tried to open the door _____ he had seen the man lock it.
11 I would rather have a cup of hot tea _____ drink a mug of cold coffee.
12 I cut my hand _____ I put a plaster on it.
13 Joe wanted to buy some sweets _____ he hadn't brought enough money.
14 I shall wear a T-shirt _____ it is a warm day.
15 The girls are going hiking _____ swimming.

Rewrite these words, drawing a line to separate the **syllables**.

Example: yellow   yel/low

16 bubble _____   17 paddle _____

18 flannel _____   19 kennel _____

20 arrive _____   21 saddle _____

22 burrow _____   23 cabbage _____

Complete this table of comparing **adjectives**.

24–31

	add 'er'	add 'est'
short		
high		
small		
slow		

Circle the silent letter in each of these words.

32 scene   33 discipline

34 fascinate   35 crescent

With a line, match the words that have the same letter string (group of letters) but which make a different sound.

36 snow   have
37 pull   trough
38 ear   skull
39 wave   cow
40 bough   wear

Now go to the Progress Chart to record your score!   Total   40

Paper 17

Billy Doesn't Like School Really

Billy doesn't like school really.
It's not because he can't do the work
but because some of the other kids
don't seem to like him that much.

They call him names
and make up jokes about his mum.

Everyone laughs ... except Billy.
Everyone laughs ... except Billy.

They all think it's OK
because it's only a laugh and a joke
and they don't really mean it anyway
but Billy doesn't know that.

Billy doesn't know that
and because of that
Billy doesn't like school really.

by Paul Cookson

Underline the right answers.

1. Does Billy like school?
   (yes, no, don't know)

2. How many children don't like Billy?
   (all of them, some of them, none of them)

Answer these questions.

3. Who doesn't laugh in this poem?

   _____

4–5. What two things do the other children do to Billy?

   (1) _____

   (2) _____

6 Why do all the children think it is OK to have a laugh and a joke?

_____

7–9 Write three words describing how you would feel if you were Billy.

_____   _____   _____

Write the two small words each **compound word** is made from.

10 handbag   =   _____ + _____

11 sunlight   =   _____ + _____

12 candlestick = _____ + _____

13 shoelace   =   _____ + _____

14 toothpaste =   _____ + _____

15 dustbin   =   _____ + _____

16 postbox   =   _____ + _____

Write these words, depending on their **prefix**, in the table below.

deflate   replay   demist   prehistoric   revisit   precaution

17–22

re	de	pre

Write each of these **phrases** in a sentence and don't forget the missing apostrophe.

23–24 this birds chicks

_____

25–26 that girls sweets

_____

27–28 those boys pencils

_____

Antony likes outdoor games; he is very popular with the other boys, and he is untidy and noisy. Brian is artistic and he likes making things. He is neat and quiet.

Underline the correct sentences.

29–33 Antony likes playing football.
Brian's books are not very tidy.
Brian likes painting.
Antony is a quiet, tidy boy.
Brian likes craft lessons.
The other boys like Antony.
Antony would rather do woodwork than play cricket.
Brian is often told he must not make so much noise.
Antony would rather play cricket than stay indoors.

Copy any **nouns**, **adjectives**, **verbs** and **adverbs** found in the sentence below.

34–40 While walking briskly on a windy Thursday I heard a loud scream.

nouns _____

adjectives _____

verbs _____

adverbs _____

Now go to the Progress Chart to record your score! Total 40

Paper 18

A long time ago there lived a poor barber. The barber was poor because not enough people seemed to want their hair cut or their beards trimmed. This was the fashion at the time. The barber's wife was always complaining that she didn't have enough to eat. She would say to her husband, 'If you did not have enough money to support a wife, why did you marry me? When I was in my father's house I had plenty to eat, but here there is never anything in the larder.' Then she would take a broom and beat the poor barber until his back was quite blue.

One day, the barber was so stung by his wife's words – not to mention the broom – that he decided to leave the house and vowed never to return until he became rich. He packed a bag and set off, trudging the road from village to village, until he came to the edge of a forest. His feet ached, so he lay down in the shade of a tall tree to bemoan his hard lot. 'I must be the most unhappy barber in the land,' he moaned, 'perhaps in the whole world.'

As the barber said this, something stirred in the branches of the tree above him. You see, this tree was the home of a ghost, and ghosts don't like people coming near their territory. As the ghost floated down, it spread its long white arms and stood like a tall palm tree before the barber, its gaping mouth hanging wide open. 'Barber, you must suffer for disturbing me,' cried the ghost. 'I am going to destroy you, you miserable person.'

The barber had never seen a ghost before, so he behaved as most people do when they first see one. His legs shook and the hair on his head stood straight up like the bristles on his wife's broom. But although he was frightened, the barber kept his head. 'Oh, ghostly spirit,' he said through chattering teeth, 'I wonder whether you will destroy me when I show you what I have in my bag?'

'Stupid barber,' replied the ghost, 'how can the contents of your bag prevent me destroying you?' But he was an inquisitive ghost too, and he added, 'Let me see what you have in your bag; then I will strike you dead.'

The barber slowly opened his bag. 'I hardly dare to say this to you, ghost, but my bag is full of ghosts I have captured during the last few days. In fact, there is barely room for one more ghost in here before I take them home for my good wife to make into ghost soup. When I have captured you, ghost, and squeezed you into my bag, I'll be on my way.' So saying, the barber took from his bag the mirror he used to enable his customers to see whether their beards had been trimmed to their taste.

From *Ghost Soup* by John Paton

Underline the right answers.

1 The barber was unsuccessful because of (his lack of skill, the low price for cutting hair, the fashion for longer hair and beards).

2 The barber's wife was angry because (she wanted to stay with her father, she did not have enough clothes, she did not have enough to eat).

3 The ghost looked like (a black shape, a white sheet, a palm tree).

Answer these questions.

4–5 Give two reasons why the barber left home.

(1) _____

(2) _____

6 Why was the ghost angry with the barber?

_____

7 Describe what happened to the barber's body when the ghost spoke to him.

_____

8 What is meant by 'the barber kept his head' in line 26?

_____

9 What do you think the barber's plan was?

_____

_____

Underline the **noun** or nouns in each sentence which use the same word in their **plural** and **singular** form.

10 The aircraft flew high in the sky.

11–12 The dressmaker used her scissors to cut the fabric for the clothes.

13 The tourists watched the bison from their coach.

14 The steep Welsh slopes are home to the sheep.

Circle the ous words that have been spelt correctly.

15–20   poisonous   couragous   curious

jealous   hideous   dangeous

serrious   humorous

tremendous

Put a question mark or exclamation mark at the end of each sentence.

21 Catch the thief_____

22 Shall we look in this shop_____

23 Don't do that_____

24 Why does Dad snore so loudly_____

25 Can we go swimming now_____

26 Hurry up, time is running out_____

27 Listen, a siren_____

28 Please may I have a sweet_____

Circle the words that wouldn't have been widely used a hundred years ago.

29–34 camcorder   DVD player   donkey
cinema   doctor   astronaut   television
candle   microwave   cloth

Put the **pronouns** in the correct columns in the table.

me   yours   hers   I   mine   theirs

35–40

Pronouns about others	Pronouns about myself

Now go to the Progress Chart to record your score!   Total   40

Paper 19

A witness's report on the robbery

It was about 5.20 pm, though I can't be sure of the exact time. My watch is a few minutes fast. I was walking down Nelson Street on my way to the bus stop. There were not many people around. The shops were getting ready to close and the streetlights were starting to come on. I was hurrying for the bus but must have missed it, as there was no one waiting at the stop.

I just stopped to tie my shoelace up when I saw two men come by. I looked at them carefully, for some reason. It was something about the way they behaved. They looked nervous. One of the men was quite tall. He was wearing a raincoat and blue jeans. I can't remember the colour of his hair but do remember that he couldn't keep his hands still. He must have been about 35 or 40. The other man was shorter, and in his twenties I'd say. He had a blue baseball cap on, with the word 'Italy' written on it. He didn't look very Italian to me, he was too fair. He was whispering to the tall man, who was still fidgeting. The men seemed like they were waiting for someone or something. They were outside Smithards the jewellers. The lights were still on inside, but I could see the assistants starting to take the rings, brooches and watches out of the window, so they must have been about to close.

The men stood there for a moment, looking uncertain what to do. Then the tall man said 'Now!' He must have said it quite loudly, because I'm a bit deaf and I definitely heard it.

Immediately the men ran towards the shop and burst through the door. There was a shout from inside, then some screams. An alarm started to go off somewhere. It was incredibly loud and before I knew what was happening I heard police sirens coming up the street. Just then the men came crashing out of the shop. The tall man in the baseball cap was carrying a bag in his hand. As they tumbled into the street, they saw the police cars and just ran for it as fast as they could.

Underline the right answers.

1 The witness was (shopping, coming home from work, going to catch a bus).

2 The two men looked (untidy, nervous, hurried, frightened).

3 It was (daylight, morning, night, twilight).

Answer these questions.

4 What does the taller man do that shows he was nervous?

_____

5 How did the witness know the shop was about to close?

_____

6–7 List two things that the witness was not sure about.

_____

_____

8 The witness seems to have made a mistake in describing the men when they came out of the shop. What was it?

_____

_____

Add the missing commas in each sentence.

9–10 Aman has to buy carrots potatoes rice and tomatoes at the shop.

11–13 At the park Geri Meena David Jason and John all play together.

14–15 On Mark's way to school he passes the police station the swimming pool the park and the shops.

16–17 At the farm the children fed the goats stroked the pigs milked the cows and brushed the horse.

Complete this table of comparing **adjectives**. Some words need their last letter doubled before adding the **suffix**.

18–25

	add 'er'	add 'est'
hot		
tall		
big		
thin		

Complete each word to make a **diminutive**.

        ling   let   ock

26 drop_____   27 duck_____

28 bull_____   29 book_____

Write this sentence again, adding the missing punctuation and capital letters.

30–35 max asked is it time jess got out of bed

_____

_____

Write *their* or *there* in each of the spaces below. Don't forget to start with a capital letter if necessary.

36 The children went to play with _____ friends in the swimming pool.

37 _____ isn't going to be any rain today.

38–39 _____ shoes are over _____ on the floor.

40 _____ was a huge bang as the fireworks exploded.

Now go to the Progress Chart to record your score!   Total   40

Paper 20

A Smuggler's Song

If you wake at midnight, and hear a horse's feet
Don't go drawing back the blind, or looking in the street,
Them that asks no questions isn't told a lie.
Watch the wall, my darling, while the Gentlemen go by!
Five and twenty ponies
Trotting through the dark –
Brandy for the Parson,
'Baccy for the Clerk;
Laces for a lady, letters for a spy,
And watch the wall, my darling, while the Gentlemen go by!

Running round the woodlump if you chance to find
Little barrels, roped and tarred, all full of brandy-wine,
Don't you shout to come and look, nor use 'em for your play.
Put the brushwood back again – and they'll be gone next day!
If you see the stable-door setting open wide,
If you see a tired horse lying down inside;
If your mother mends a coat cut about and tore;
If the lining's wet and warm – don't you ask no more!

From *A Smuggler's Song* by Rudyard Kipling

Underline the right answers.

1 Which of these things does the poem tell you to do?

(draw back the blind, look out in the street, ask no questions, shout out if you find barrels)

2 Who are the Gentlemen?

(soldiers, smugglers, rich men, lords)

3 What are the barrels covered with?

(coats, brushwood, straw, grass)

Answer these questions.

4 What time would the smugglers be likely to come?

_____

5 What things might the smugglers bring?

_____

6 Why does the poem tell you to watch the wall?

_____

7 What are the barrels secured with?

_____

8 How can you tell this poem is written to a child rather than a grown-up?

_____

Add the **suffix** *ship* or *hood* to each of these words.

9 friend_____   10 neighbour_____

11 mother_____   12 apprentice_____

Add *its* or *it's* to fill the gap in each sentence. Don't forget to start with a capital letter if necessary.

13 _____ a beautiful day.

14 The cat played with _____ ball.

15–16 _____ time you remembered your own bag, _____ not that hard!

17 Everyone was lined up outside the school; _____ fire alarm was going.

18 Will's dog lost _____ ball.

19 _____ got to be here somewhere!

20 _____ been a brilliant party. I wish I could have one every week!

Write a **phrase** (group of words) that could describe each of these **nouns**.

Example: bed   the soft, feathery, comfortable bed

21 **coat** _____

22 **elephant** _____

23 **car** _____

24 **skyscraper** _____

25 **tree** _____

26 **egg** _____

27 **flower** _____

Use one of the following **conjunctions** in each gap.

         but   and   so   after   because

28 I missed the train _____ I overslept.

29 Ahmed is in the cricket team _____ Josh wasn't good enough.

30 Mum wrapped up my present _____ I went to bed.

31 Jake bought some toffees _____ Mike got some too.

32 Cathy's sewing is untidy _____ she will have to do it again.

33 I like macaroni _____ my brother likes spaghetti better.

34 The sky was blue _____ the sun was shining.

Match the words to their **definitions**.

soon sleepy error cautious herd adult

35 group of cattle _____

36 grown-up _____

37 heavy-eyed _____

38 careful _____

39 mistake _____

40 in a short time _____

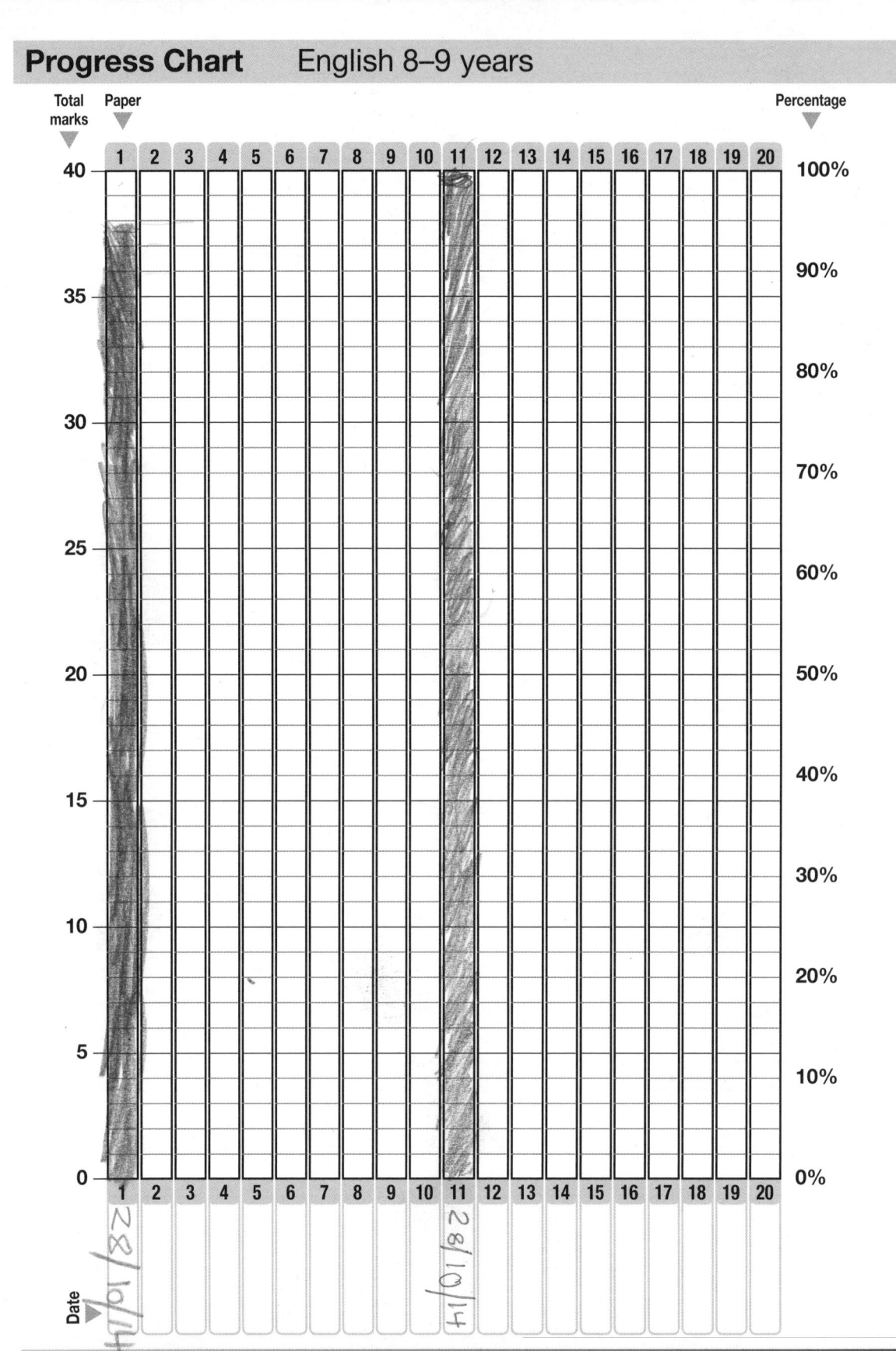

Progress Chart — English 8–9 years

Paper	Total marks	Date
1	~38	28/10/14
11	~40	28/10/14

When you've finished the book read the Next Steps